Little Universe

Natalie Ann Holborow is a winner of the Terry Hetherington Award and the Robin Reeves Prize and has been shortlisted and commended for the Bridport Prize, the National Poetry Competition, the Hippocrates Prize for Poetry and Medicine, and the Cursed Murphy Spoken Word Award among others. Her writing residencies with the British Council, Literature Wales and Kultivera have seen her writing and performing poetry in Wales, Ireland, Sweden and India. She is the author of the poetry collections *And Suddenly You Find Yourself* and *Small* – both listed as Best Poetry Collections of the Year by *Wales Arts Review* – and, with Mari Ellis Dunning, the collaborative poetry pamphlet *The Wrong Side of the Looking Glass*. *Little Universe* is her third full collection. Natalie lives in Swansea, is a proud patron of local charity The Leon Heart Fund and runs marathons to raise funds.

natalieholborow.com

Little Universe

Natalie Ann Holborow

PARTHIAN

Parthian, Cardigan SA43 1ED www.parthianbooks.com
First published in 2024
© Natalie Ann Holborow 2024
ISBN 978-1-917140-21-8
Editor: Susie Wildsmith
Cover design by Emily Courdelle
Typeset by Elaine Sharples
Printed and bound by 4edge Limited, UK
Published with the financial support of the Books Council of Wales
British Library Cataloguing in Publication Data
A cataloguing record for this book is available from the British Library
Printed on FSC accredited paper

Little Universe is provided to selected libraries across Wales with support of The Borzello
Trust to promote the reading of contemporary poetry by new and emerging voices.

For Dad and Em

In memory of my wonderful grandad

Let your soul stand cool and composed before a million universes.
– Walt Whitman

CONTENTS

Departure

Pulse

In that recurring dream of the hospital

you're a plunging ship
in a gown that blooms around you.
The ward lights dazzle like Perseids

until you're stranded
in a room of your own,
tempered with morphine and bedrest,

moored so close to the window
I'm terrified to look in, the view
alarmingly blue and upside-down.

Though you are sinking
your arm waves to me
like wet laundry,

your face neutral,
primed for the blow.

The Medical Students

They stored up bedsheets like unsent post,
muffled gossip into linen, watched the colours of sickness
skid into the observation ward like kidnapped dogs.

Mrs P had a cyst the size of a swelling papaya.
Mr K gnashed through the morphine; veins spiralled with wire.
To observe was to stand back in terrified awe and know

every one of us is fucked. Miss O with too many shadows came next,
her cough spilled sour with pills. Quietly, the students strode
marathons in rubber shoes, splitting a sea through the ward.

Little did they know, their stethoscopes bright,
how these wounds would stitch up invisibly,
scars running the length of their lives.

Elevator

In the department store
she asks me if he's *really* okay
as she tugs a coat from the rails
swings the hem about her calves
hands burrowing through tunnels
of faux-satin lining searching
for an answer she can believe
while I'm staring at the mirror
handbag clamped beneath my armpit
thinking of an acceptable response
while somewhere a drip-stand
of slow fluid tries to revive him
the changing-room curtains too dark
my soft-pelted sister
tramps her way to the elevator
her walk a windsweep of nausea
the metal doors snap behind us
not knowing what's on the next floor
or what we're expecting to find there.

Family Therapy

What if we only showed ourselves half-revealed
in photographs, as if to draw any closer
to each other could give us away in a thunderclap.
Rearranging those pixels of light you'd find
your own features in another's expression

until you come to recognise its clandestine angles,
the way shadows flower the cheek on a hair's-breadth,
loose enough to pull. Perhaps then we'll learn
it might always have been more than a waiting room
in which none of us could hold out long enough,

those stiff teardrops of time, a parachute of feathers
exploding from the night, too soon to roost on expressions
held secret, the faces that fit yours precisely.

On Most or All of the Days

Are you startled to find your own body
        blotchy with shame and birdshit, a marching sarcophagus
banging the door behind you?

Is your office chair unable to stand
        the weight of you? Does your headrest
thump jokingly at your skull?

Can you sometimes smell
        your own sleeplessness like iron, smoke,
a mouthful of scorched stars?

Does the shower turn its head in disgust?
        Does your arm treble in weight before waving
and every handshake collapse in your fist?

Recovered

I told you I was recovered,
fingers squeezed
around the nib of a toothpick

pierced a shining olive
watched it bleed
misty oil

beneath my dress
the clattering rib, valves
pouring, a sudden clasp

at the meaty ventricles, you reddened
your lips with wine,
tore a strip of lamb between your teeth

while I pretended to swallow mine.

Self-help

1.
I plant two seeds of Fluoxetine in my stomach
        that flower from my throat as bittercress.

2.
I try to journal, swirling the ink into a formal complaint.

3.
I write a letter, addressed to God
        with a conglomeration of fines for damages.

4.
I scroll furiously, searching for God's current home address.
        Google thoughtfully flashes up an ad for self-help.

5.
I make phone calls to two archangels
        hanging up as soon as they say *hello.*

6.
I remember about caller ID.

7.
I swallow two more green-and-white seeds,
        say *wait* to the sparrows warbling my name.

8.
I open my throat wide, hoping this time for sunflowers.

Physiotherapy

She knows your body
in a way no one else does,

     instructs you to take a step
         as though it were a tango move
you can't get right

on feet that have danced
         an avalanche of patterns
the tiles now make too ordinary.

The last thing you'd thought
you'd dare yourself to do

     would be to *slow down*
         as you crank yourself
    like a stiff ballerina
         unfolding from a music-box
towards the ninth floor window,

legs jaunting
    in slow motion,
         the long clear-pane stretch

        you now flail for,
    her hand orbiting your waist,

protecting your centre of gravity.

Balancing Act

3.7 mmol
Beside the bed, a bright heap of gummy bears
tumble out of the packet like aliens, landing in lamplight.
I take one, lurid green, lean into the haze,
topple a glass, darken the carpet that drags me
shivering into its currents.

5.5 mmol
Briefly, my body is a perfect machine, elated
by this fleeting sense of balance, circulating
what needs to be shifted. The rain
that runs at everything has never felt so clean
as it does now, dancing off my fingers,
filling the throats of tulips, red and sweet.

18.2mmol
Like dunking your head upside-down
into warm bathwater or trying to open
your eyes in the wind. Left long enough
suspended in molasses, slowly percolating,
I'll pour rivers into the rasp of my gullet,
shrug myself yawning off the bone.

1.8mmol
In the pool changing room of all places,
freezing and nude, scrabbling for orange juice.
The straw stabs hopelessly for the little foil circle.
Wet hair dangling like ropes, drips oozing
down my neck – some clear, some fulgent orange,
some of them trembling with salt.

How to Cure a Hypo

I blink down at a fistful of grapes
someone brought as a gift. Pluck each one
from its stem in a spinning room, burst
a mouthful of summer between my teeth.

Sweat and shivers have stilled all thoughts
except the one that tells me to eat, manoeuvres
my fingers from bowl to mouth, green
explosions of fructose chilling the throat.

When I grab the final branch sunlight plumps
my pillows, grapes popping, shuttling
juiced sweetness from throat to stomach,
reviving my blood's slow orbit.

Unseasonable Winds

The scar on your hand throbs,
recalling wire, fingers shaped

in the curl of my detonating fist.
Somewhere in the clementine sky

    a light is trying to spill

and I'm terrified you'll lift off
in unseasonable winds,

your name and address
etched along a wristband

    as though I could ever forget them.

The Porter

And without thinking, my tattooed hands are shunting
a precarious wheelchair, awoken by its heaviness.
A door lies back for me to enter and a patient crawls
from its eye. She asks me how I came to be working here
and I tell her the job is good, that the people are nice,
carefully omitting how some stories weigh more than others,
how some corridors stretch further than ever expected
and how sometimes we hear hurricanes roar
in the wheels that rattle ahead of us.

Hypoglycaemia

A fever muffles around a dream and turns
cold. Under strip lights lie slabs of bread
stiffening in bags, the steady buzz
of a greenbottle, its persistence against clingfilm.
I sink my knife uselessly into butter, jar, drag the blade
between my teeth. A sigh of fly and honey.
My first hypo in weeks, I prise lids
with shaking fingers. Sugar snows into my palm,
shivering and sweet.

Waiting Room at the Breast Clinic

Gowns yanked across our chests,
we're startled butterflies dropping
into plastic chairs, terrified to weigh
our fears against the dead clock

where optimism is a dawn of pistachio
wall paint smoothing years
of contained panic, leaflets pulled taut

in fidgety hands. A breast slips to the side
and is re-bundled, with all the shame
of a stolen apple.

A door judders, knocking our gaze
sideways. And then the next name –
a chair scrapes,

the patient's footsteps wading
as though under the sea,
not knowing the current's direction.

Rescue

Behind the door, the doctor scrawls her notes –
fingers slouching off with the pen between her fingers
until suddenly
        she's descending
                the precarious escalator
                        of someone's spine,
            then breezing back again
to lift her head, sip coffee, her hair
a snarl of wisps and vibrissa,

for a moment intimately acquainted with a face
she'd looked upon briefly, the look she'd seen

on the boy tucked into himself foetally,
plasters wrinkling his elbows

so that when she drops her head again
        her hand is already swimming in reverse

to find him, clawing him back from the light.

Inhale

Tell it to the trees

when summer strides off with its head
hanging bright as a lemon, the closing heaven
giving way to a bloat of lavender clouds
the oak with its crown of copper bending low –
its branches would clutch for the mud of your heart
if it could, moss peppering the wood,
its mind ruffling with crows.

Tell it to the trees
to the branches cupped in your open palm
blooming to sudden angles, pale as candles
melting down, a swell of leaves unlatching
in the last of the yellow afternoon
when the sun is a shrinking balloon
untethered from your grasp, when the clouds
unclasp and the dark earth steams with drizzle.

Tell it to the trees
that familiar breeze whipping the hazel bare
raking each strand of your hair skyward
there's a certain moment of quiet
that can only emerge from the wild.
Those red leaves go on raining
to soothe what's reeling inside.

Into Gŵyr

Each summer an echo of summers past,
an after-image washed by the shore –
castles, wet footprints, a bunker
dissolving to gold upon Pennard's shoulder.

The cool Atlantic sloshes higher, closer
than lavender, the surrendering dusk folds
into sleep on Rhossili. The peppering bell heather,
goldilocks aster striking cliff-edge to fire –

its untouchable litmus of smoke
where we arrive, not like strangers
but easing back, sweeping the century's current,
noting each pure and tiny thing –

the bee's drunken wingbeat
drilling hours among the orchids
silk-seamed, that familiar braid of sea
unstitching itself along Oxwich.

On Llanmadoc, trees rake themselves
brown across marshes,
a slow snowfall of curlews,
breeze whipped to a slippery hush.

Around them, ponies carousel,
trample their startled applause.

Claiming Oxwich Castle

Today we're claiming Oxwich castle, waging war
in the wrong direction, shadows catching the giveaway
ribbons of nylon scarves, the trailing worm of your bootlace
while you're framing imagined breastplates with your fingers,
leaning an arm against the archway, polyester-jacketed knight
measuring almost horse-height, a cotton bloom opening red
where you clipped your ankle scrambling the fence,
refusing to pay entry, a modern-day Owain Glyndŵr
putting on an accent, forgetting the way your tongue
stumbles, too casual, over the rolling *R*.

The Cockle Women of Penclawdd

Rushing towards them and away again
this pulse of water is never still,
sometimes a silvered blade in the mudflats
sometimes freezing, ankle-gorged.
The cockle women are wading
out to their ankles, skirts hitched,
baskets hunkered to their spines,
boots plunged into sludge and cordgrass.
The sun has not yet warmed the marshes
as they move in half-darkness, following
a shift in the water's trajectory.
Bent double, backsides pushed against the sky,
the women scrabble, raking cockles from sand
with quick pulls to riddle them free from their beds.
Donkeys shivering at their sides, hooves thrust against
the swell of glutted sacks, shells clattering, those glittering molluscs
sometimes squirming, sometimes rattling with sand,
empty where nature had got there first.

Anemones

Built for bracing emergencies, they squat below
sea level, tinselled cilia outstretched, dying
to be brushed by fishtails, whale bellies,
the curious human finger

drawn to those skinny red hairs. Like any
devious flower – *aconitum, rafflesia, oleander* –
dark is calloused in toxic places,
splits the sudden blade of light

probed by the diver's lamp. Invaders
will be buried with their bulbs and flippers
until anemones blossom from eye sockets,
flagellate from slackened jaws, find foothold

in a gloss of disjointed icesheets. Later
they'll turn in revolt from shipwrecks,
splayed gull bones, a dark ceiling of plastic
rings panned like trawler nets, waiting to tighten.

Guillemots

It's the way the water doesn't just meet the shore
but rushes at it, slung with rags of seaweed
as though it simply passed out from the joy of it all.

Sometimes, I think of landslides
as those soft, yielding parts of us, exposed,
wind guttering our throats.

Strange, how the landscape
shapes us.

How currents return us
towards the warm, dark centre
of our own wilderness, how guillemots
rumble above as though ready to plunge

like comets into our laps.

On Not Writing

You know that sudden urge: to say something
about the bees clanging between bluebells,

to scull your palms through a wave's raw edges
and tug it upshore like a sheet,

to wring something out of it.

How long have you been here,
a whole ocean at your back, resisting?

The woods are silent, exhaling birds
and nothing is ready to answer.

Not the fishing boat rocked on a slick of breeze,
nor the mackerel thrashing iron-bright,
their tails sliding off your fingers,

tiny wet mouths popping,
kissing the air as they go.

Mountain Song

A damp wind off the cliff-edge
is music dismantled; low, chill
on limestone.

> *Y Mynydd Du*
> in monochrome, its valleys
> spreading like curtains

where back and forth on the Skirrid
a shadow goes loping forever
squeezing mountains to its chest.

> A poem is a river unbraided.
> Here, in the bone-cold air
> a waterfall quietly unstitches itself

in the first of the swelling light.
A sheep pauses mid-mouthful,
coat pearled with dew.

> Clouds sag like wet muslin.
> It is for this they push on,
> veiling the hillsides,

unravelling to smoke
but still moving
like those brilliant glaciers

> shunting back into winter
> or the throat of the red wind opening,
> shaking the church bells awake.

Send Nothing This Year

21st June 2020

We were holding each other carefully
on a cracked screen, at arm's length
like a precious hawk, just spreading.

That night, I dreamt I was asphyxiated in a bee-suit,
where to show compassion is to step back, wait
in a tree's cool cavity for the other to pass. Remember

each other's birthdays, send nothing this year
but a text. One sneeze followed by another,
clamping the jaw safely, mouth covered.

How wearily you pull Kleenex from the packet,
stick figures springing backwards into hedgerows,
snowing pollen. How the world might not swallow you back.

Spring Tide

The farmers here say their ewes know the tides,
that when it tops seven metres, the lambing
will start and the farmers will tear from their pillows.

It's their hooves, they say – the moisture rising
through samphire, sea thrift, fescue, darkening wool
like days-old bandages, telling the body to push.

The breath holds behind the teeth, estuary swollen,
the womb paused mid-squeeze, and yet here I am,
thinking of those waiting sheep

as I sit in the car park outside Maternity,
my sister somewhere inside
having sweated and punched for hours,

barely noticing the water that's heaved itself
up to her window, spilling fresh salt over the tiles.

Exhale

Companion Moons

My phone illuminates – a photograph of my sister
weeping over the wet, purplish heap of her son
moments after his entrance.

The bulge of his heel kicks at the air,
still trying to find a foothold
in the borders of her belly,
squirming plumply in the camera's flare.

Suitably distanced, my sister and I
revolve on our pillows like companion moons,
align one's relief to the other.

Little Universe

For Leo

Every morning, he chants the planets
as though in prayer, rolling plastic spheres
until they align across his bedroom rug.
For hours he kneels tight-lipped,
nudging Jupiter back into orbit,
rolling Mars across synthetic wool.
Clasping Earth in his pudgy hands he lifts it up,
taps at the green, inspects its brilliance. Puzzling
the solar system, he taps each planet as he goes,
putting order back into his bright little universe.

The Push

Just off the lane from the entrance
long sloughed to a rubbled stump

the young girls squirm through the fence.
Tiny, barely ten years between them

they stagger forwards as though emerging
from sleep, hands smacked to their mouths,

thrilled by the tyre swing, its silent rope.
I want to tell them to turn around,

to save themselves
from microscopic hazards

where other hands have touched –
but for now, watching them

break the rules, grip the cord,
one girl pushing the other, what I wish

is to savour the look on her sister's face,
the locks of her hair whirled skywards,

to forget that this, too,
is an act of danger.

Pebbling

The day is an aria, its light a familiar gift
in which my nephew pads towards the toybox,
sails a plastic ark over the laminate. Plucking out creatures,
he queues up tiny pairs beside the plastic boat, muted
waves unscrolling into a small-scale flood.

When he presses a plastic giraffe into my sister's hand,
a sudden seriousness clouding his face, she calls it *pebbling*,
translates his silent palming of precious objects
into something like *love you, too*.

Microchimerism

Once pregnant, they say you'll always carry
a piece of your baby's DNA – the cells
shifting from one body to the other.
I like to think that's why my heart thumps
when my nephew's spongy hand sits snug as a plum
in mine or how something breaks in me
when he looks up, says *moon*, lips pushed forward
as though trying to drink its milky light.
My body knows something no one else does,
has harboured what didn't stand a chance.
We carry our secret through supermarkets,
drift among the fruit, pausing for a moment
to feel six pounds of honeydew cradled in our arms.

The Problem

There's a lot that will be expected of you.
First, everyone will assume it's you
who is the problem.

They'll lean in to hear the static of your nerves
as they explain about follicles, eggs, tubes,
cysts swelling like sea-sponges –

any part of your complex machinery
that could fail. The phlebotomist's finger
will dig at a stubborn vein, pull blood

in deep, inky gulps. You'll say you don't smoke,
rarely drink, multiply your five a day,
then unravel on a plastic sheet.

Thigh-deep in light, you'll feel the dye
sweep through fallopian tubes,
uterus blown tight as a water-balloon.

Sympathetic women at your ankles,
patting uselessly. They'll talk about
ripening, harvesting,

how to con the seasons of your body
with Clomid, follicle stimulating hormones,
needles diving into your belly,

and you'll wish that the only thing expected of you
is to jack off into a coffee cup
then count the winning numbers.

Thawing

As the candle blows out he warms her bones, presses
a fresh mug of tea in her hand. It's something, to defrost
from the inside out, to have been thawed by love,
blowing smoke signals across the cup.

When she catches herself in the oven's reflection
it's the belly she reimagines, blown to a drum,
catching the blink of a tea-drop as it rolls.
The breasts swollen in their cups.

To warm is to nurture. He tips the teapot
into a curtsey, holds the delicate handle
steady. He wants the steam to wrap them lightly
until the worst of love is over,
to feel it shivering as it goes.

Fetch

Dark rump wriggling into the chasm
between cereal cupboard and dryer,
Ted's on a mission to retrieve
remnants of the rented life before us:
gum wrappers, odd socks, a yolk-yellow
Kinder case devoid of its prize.
He squirms out, bottom-first,
a single jelly shoe
clamped between his teeth.

His best day had him nudging half a coconut
across the tiles, tail walloping, announcing the kill.
This purge reaffirms itself in crumbled flowerbeds,
airing cupboards and washing lines
as we contemplate his treasures,
the brittle peg cracking between his jaws
a catalyst of false retrospection.

Pumpkin

I lift it like a plump child:
this year's pumpkin. Autumn's moon
resplendent, shining with pulp.

With a cough of seeds, a smile
carved out with nonchalant ease,
I have stolen somebody's head.

Stooped at the doorstep, I strike night
into fire, smoke, gourd-rind,
cup the thrashing wick with my fingers.

This huge warm crown my trophy:
here is the skull of a make-believe man;
head tumbled clean from his shoulders.

Anchored on the doorstep:
a beaming dream, my intruder
with a smile lit hot as a planet.

Demeter

The wind bites like iced water: howling, tearless,
a caduceus-cramp of grief, each springing horizon
of sheafs, blowsy chaffs, irrevocably rucked.

Daughter of darkness, I'm flinging half-moons
to find you. I'm reversing the harvest's abundance,
flattening tracks, excavating the world's core
like some terrible fruit, culling coal
in the scoop of my fists. My daughter of slime
and shingle, lovelorn, growing thinner,
eye battened on the white of Hades' skull:
a low wolf-whistle through the eyehole.

A funeral-song, no tune. My daughter waltzed
to the Underworld, festooned in flame.
Queen of disintegration, observing the dead
as they lie with a sourness in their mouths.
Their bones briefly lifting in the rising of the Styx.

Lilith

Once he'd obscured the gates to Paradise
with marigolds, nasturtiums, apple blossom,
and left the bars too thin for human structures;
when he cast the woman out, bare-breasted,

Adam tight-lipped beside her, missing
a stipple of rib, God stood there for two, three
minutes before he saw me, striding in huge
elastic movements, a shore of thundering losses.

Let me tell you this, my darling Eve
(I shine the apple of her cheek
as I speak), do not lie beneath him
when he asks. Offer nothing, speak

loud enough to let Mother Earth
hear every word, become a crypt
of stubborn roots. And when he pulls,
test your diction against the birds,

swallow their language, learn something
he won't know then stun him with it.
It could take the birth of one demon,
or the agony of hundreds,

their red cries splitting the earth,
but listen, swallow knowledge
from one woman to another:

man will summon thighs
from serpents' bodies, rewrite ours,
say anything to save his burning skin.

Run Like a Girl

Only every other streetlight works, so for each dark shutter
there's a surprise abyss opening beneath her,
a languid sheet of sweat developing at her neck,
heels skimming the dirt, battering the draught
of whatever she's running from this time
only she's at her checkpoint already, toes scuffing the world.

Car horns don't keep her – she constructs a rocket of herself,
launches the other way, shadows clambering the hems
of her patterned shorts, ponytail Catherine-wheeling,
always facing the violent headlights,
hoping for tailwinds behind her.

Paris

He pauses to smooth his hair in the rear-view mirror
of the 4x4 he's straddled across two spaces, a 340-horsepower
engine he's nursed around the car park for fifteen minutes,
unusually early. Appointment letter crunched in his fist,
knuckling dread, a packet of cigarettes for the wait ahead.

Fifteen minutes pass blowing battle-cries into smoke-clouds,
wheezing out some deeper pain, holding out at the door
for as long as his name takes to summon him in,
rusty arrow pushing through the shoulder's plane of skin,
wolf-whistling his way through reception.

Later, he'll sit upon tomato-red plastic, yank up his sleeve,
await the sting. Torchlight dazzling his eyes to check he's in.

Europa

Pierce Europa's 15-mile-deep
skin of ice and we might find
an ocean grinding beneath it
twice as low as the Earth's floor
and if scientists think that life
can exist in such impossibly
dark places breathing out
as though to melt snow
or clean a forgotten mirror
imagine what could go on living
miraculously behind these walls
like lucky astronauts
thump-landing onto
a resplendent moon.

Treacle

I'm useless at the paltry shelves
of the hospital tuck shop, looking for something
my grandfather might eat. A sticky Mars, a bag of nuts,
an orange sucking in on itself –
nothing good enough.

I want to ask them to stock sticky pudding tins,
let him taste that one sweet thing
that won't sear his shining throat,
his eyes closed in pleasure
against the warmth of treacled spoons.

Departure

Checking Out

The rain steams away the end
of the corridor you trespass at midnight,
that slow milky froth that spreads in the chill.

A doorstep, a warning, a bed of wet geraniums.

So many reasons it's easier to keep walking,
to cough smoke-wreaths outside entrances,
to find your car waiting, frozen.

An ambulance backs up in slow motion.

Across the car park two stars meet
then shear away without touching.

A Student Returns

You enter the shut classroom –
its rusty hinges bat-squeaking
against your shoulder.

Breath snuffs the window,
you smiling with grim fascination
at that buckled skeleton, the last
ragged flutter of a doctor's coat
dangling from its sternum.

Hips, sulphur-yellow, pocked
with scratches after years of being shunted
from lecture to lecture. Moth caterpillars
thudding plumply from a severed arm.

But you can't let go can you?
Touching its fingers tenderly, measuring
your hand against a plastic metacarpus,
convinced it'll squeeze you back.

You Won't Always Recognise Hope
When You See Her

Sometimes she's hunched in the visitors' room
rolling a magazine into a baton, thumping her thigh
like a labrador-tail, waiting for someone to show.
Sometimes she's stretched tenderly across the bed,
fingers crowding her mother's wrist, interrogating the blood
for movement. And sometimes she's outside
spinning coils of smoke like prayers into the bitter air,
light crawling across her brow, angling her phone for signal.
Maybe you missed her, ankle-deep, footprints engulfed by the saltmarsh
her mother's hand cream not quite laundered from her glove.
Suppose she swims to you easily over disinfected tiles,
sipping the bruised violet shine of the morning
or else she clatters in quite unexpectedly
through the vents in the hospital ceiling,
belts of seaweed wrapping her waist
to tell you the tide's come in.

Breathing Space

Look at the hands: the fingers are clutched
dark at the pine's root, twisted around an imagined cigarette.
      The sky is dragging its scarves.

None of you know who I am talking about.
None of you know that the doctor who told you to stop smoking
      is flicking a light outside Radiotherapy,

that the best-behaved patient
with the habit of long walks and eating his greens
      is tossing a lung from the ambulance

because suddenly it's on fire. And who but the nurse
with her tired mouth could say anything tonight except *we're trying*
      in a voice that carves a maze out of the corridors

so you can run off to blow your last smoke
through the window, your body unexpectedly drifting up
      and the doctor shouting out the time

as though something had stopped.

Emergency Flowers

I want to talk to the body blown to dust
      across a clutch of emergency flowers.

I want warnings twirled in genetics
      to untwist their stiffened helices

I want to zoom through a lens microscopic
      map cures along the tributaries of nerves

            I want sirens softened to bird whistles

I want angels pressing the doorway with miracles
      whacking their fists against glass

a first breath hauled from the thorax
      a last breath cupped in the palm

and sometimes

I want the low hum of strange machinery
      a throb of incalculable pulses

I want to steer myself from tragic blooms
      to a place beyond waiting

where wildflowers frill the corridors
      and nothing is an emergency.

Forget-me-not

We're condemned to live in the visitor car park
for eternity until we've exhausted these routes.
Always, the car circles. The same light, the same hours.

We stare out to a road that is always leaving us,
our shadows divided, as if distracted by something
only one of us can see. We sit like loyal dogs

watching rain spread under the wipers
where a face in the reflection is blurred,
eyes lowered. I make it smile out of habit.

So many stories that muffle or trail off
beyond hospital walls, our own limits, a hand
that absently shifts gears until noticed.

In winter, his memory will dull
to a windy rattle,
as everything, eventually, must.

Departure Lounge

In the rush of the respiratory ward
between blank masks and screeching machines

push the fine bones of those leaving – a wind of flames
licking wild at the windows, attempting resurrection.

On the floor below, a baby suckles the theatre's
white light, face crushed in surprise

and stuffed with breath, ten fingers
and ten toes scrunched against bleached air,

the terrifying ceremony of arrival
against the peace of those departing.

The Janitor is Crying in the Gents

He cries into what resilience he has left. There's a hospital
name badge swaying from a lanyard – he must
retain an air of professionalism while sobbing,
the mop bucket rattling over the bathroom floor,
frothy with dirt: a slosh of Dettol over the skidding rush
of sons and daughters, phoned urgently
to come and squeeze a hand; arms scrabbling in Resus.

The janitor is crying in the Gents,
gripping the handle, looking down through the window
to watch sunrise unpeeling the flowers
at the hospital entrance. If he were to lean out
and reach towards them dripping soap,
they would recoil at the first heavy drop,
shrug themselves back into earth.

Waiting to Say Goodbye

It's three pounds for a latte in the hospital cafe
which the woman in front of me says is a rip-off,
stooped over the counter, clicking out tens,
a puff of cotton taped to her hand
like a miniature cloud.

I'm standing in water up to my waist
but the cafe isn't flooded, it just feels like it.
Today, my head is a blasted socket
somewhere between strip lights
and a bitter flat white,

a sinking *Get Well* balloon
dragging its little string behind it
like a stupid ribbon of hope.

Afterlife

Every night a new shadow emerges from its bed, trying
to float out to sea, that long mirage stitched in the folds
of a methylene blue curtain, its ethereal pitch unreachable
as the aspirin at the bottom of your water-jug.

As it swims, you'll wonder: have you found some dark angel
circling the door, another brush with the afterlife
or just a nurse's hand softly closing the hinges?

Turnstiles

On the long drive home,
Nan sighs
in the passenger seat,
Mam curled in the back,

my grandfather already
somewhere in space
hammering asteroid belts
into turnstiles.

Strawberries

For Grandad

Outside the garden is still the garden
you waved from; face blurred by the panes
of the greenhouse. Inside, the emptiness
is inexplicable, despite the splendour
of arachnids, vines wizening to scrolls.
The strawberry bed is full of itself,
                        blistering with redness.
Only one plucked berry turns
soft on the chopping board, the first
of the season. No hunger could make me
put it anywhere near my mouth.

As though nothing has changed

Friday nights are the hardest:
      I pull two glasses from the cupboard

thinking you're still standing beside me
      cracking pistachios into a bowl

my voice chatting to you
      as though nothing has changed.

I turn to ask you *how much*,
      bottle floating over your wine glass.

It is a shock every time
      I find no one is there to reply,

just an empty bowl
      I must have put there myself

whilst everyone else
      was talking about you.

Blood Sugar

In the event of such emergencies, the sky will ring
shrill with panic, a lump of sugared moon.

A number I glanced at but stopped thinking about
will plunge onto the highway and now it's midnight
and I'm lost at a traffic light, blaming it on rushing.

Where on earth am I going, foot on the accelerator?
Against the dashboard, a red fist bursts into light.

I've lived between the body's extreme latitudes, crawled
myself dazed from the brink, forgotten over and over
my first lesson on how to drive this machine.

A prayer bead of blood-pricked fingertips
will not save me in the front seat,
fresh sweat avalanching my spine.

Sunday Morning

In the corner of the pillow is a certain space
my head falls when it's gorged with the church bells
of Sunday morning, curtains shivering out their hangovers
in strips of faux-silk, sunshine bleaching to ripeness
carving the air into cul-de-sacs, an empty driveway.

Two years later, I'm still waiting for the polite cough
of the engine as it stops, still holding out for someone
wearing my grandfather's golf shoes, cigarette
fibrous, alight in his mouth, saying *hello flower*,
emerging as a wave from the gravel's shoreline,
a curling swell back from the edge of the universe.

Who knows what he'd be thinking, padding down
to the red front door, a meteor dragging its light.
And who knows what he'd say if he saw me here,
ribs stacked into stunning angles, each tendon
a conductor of grief electrocuting the body.

Constellation

Turning, somewhere below Auriga's bright wheel
there's a sea too dark to make out the seams,
a row of lindens rustling black, the breeze
mechanical, still breathing.

Each night the window flashes up
like a brilliant cry. Quietly, I'll excuse myself
from his bedside, look up once, twice,
squint for the edge, for a pebble of light
within arm's reach, for a constellation
prickling into view, a moon skimmed off bitter shores.

Once, I half-expected his hand to unfurl
and point it out for me, 657 square degrees
of sparkling chariot, Capella trembling with fierce light.

If he could, he might have landed from some other world,
pushed a fingertip up to the glass to show me
where it's always been, where it will still be without him.

Imagine

there will come a time when you spread miles
between your skin and wet gardens, join the swell

of yawning queues at the airport, spill out into the world
that beams vehemently at you from behind the spreading curtain,

lock your home behind you. Emerge from a chilly night
on your imagined Himalayas into a blazing, taxi-choked morning,

this post monsoon day bringing smoke and frangipani, silky
chai, a crop of new miracles springing from the snow.

Notes

Demeter: The Greek goddess of agriculture and fertility, Demeter is the devoted mother of Persephone, whose abduction by Hades leads to Demeter's grief and the seasonal cycle of growth and harvest.

Europa: One of Jupiter's moons, Europa is believed to harbour a subsurface ocean beneath its icy crust, potentially holding more than twice the water found on Earth.

Into Gŵyr:
Gŵyr is the Welsh word for Gower, an area of natural beauty in South Wales.

Paris: A Trojan prince in Homer's *The Iliad*, Paris is best known for abducting Helen, which sparked the Trojan War, and for his role as a skilled but somewhat cowardly archer in the conflict.

Run Like a Girl: In a 2023 survey by Adidas, 92% of female runners reported feeling concerned for their safety.

The Cockle Women of Penclawdd: A 1916 report by the South Wales Sea Fisheries Association estimated that nearly 320 tonnes of cockles were harvested monthly in the Penclawdd area. On a typical day, around fifty women were seen working on the beaches, with each of their donkeys carrying approximately 150kg of cockles in sacks.

Acknowledgements

Acknowledgements are due to the editors of the following publications, in which some of these poems first appeared: *Poetry Wales, The Lonely Crowd* and *Black Bough*.

'Tell it to the trees' appeared as part of a film, music and video project by Geoffrey Cox at the University of Huddersfield. 'Into Gŵyr' was commissioned by Ifor ap Glyn and Dan Llewellyn Hall for Celf Coast Cymru to celebrate the 10th anniversary of the Wales Coastal Path.

This third collection was a four-year effort which I could not have finished without the support, encouragement and advice of the following people: my Salty Poets Rhys Owain Williams, Adam Sillman, Emily Vanderploeg, Alan Kellermann, Mari Ellis Dunning and Rae Howells. Thanks also to Taz Rahman, Matthew M.C. Smith, Guinevere Clark, Jeremy Dixon, Stephen Johnston, Julie Montanari, Hazel Duke, Alasdair Bater, Luke Rose-Smith, Elaine Canning, Jamie Woods, Oliver James Lomax and Inês Cunha for your ongoing kindness and support. To Ali Franks and Matthew Knight for being the best neighbours and friends.

Special thanks to Susie Wildsmith for being the best editor a poet could ask for and to the whole Parthian team for believing in me. I feel very lucky.

To Chelsey Howells for being such an incredible friend to me, and to Roisin O'Connor and Zoe Alford for being my siren gang, always.

To our Writing Women cohort for your amazing creative energy and for being such a supportive group of talented women.

To Jimmy Watkins: thank you for your energy, creativity and ongoing support – and for reminding me of the power of writing. Shoutout to your amazing Running Punks group, a group that brings running and creativity together beautifully.

To my family: Nan (for the lifelong encouragement of my writing ambitions), Mam, Dad, Chris, Claire, Matthew, Som, Elisha, Josh, and to Callum and Em who are the best siblings I could hope for.

To Ceri (the most talented photographer I know) and Dai Llewellyn. Shoutout to his friend John for inspiring the 'Spring Tide' poem.

To Ted, my pup who has me exploring more of Gower than I've ever done before. However, I have absolutely no thanks for eating three poems while I was putting them in order.

To my lovely Ian, sorry I'm such a pain to live with when I'm up to my eyeballs in edits and burn the potato wedges. Love you always. (Chips are in the bottom freezer drawer, by the way.)

Finally, to Grandad who supported me so much with my writing – this book is for you. Miss and love you always.

Nature ticks on outside the window:
An interview with Natalie Ann Holborow

Photo by Ceri Llewellyn

Natalie Ann Holborow is a winner of the Terry Hetherington Award and the Robin Reeves Prize and has been shortlisted and commended for the Bridport Prize, the National Poetry Competition, the Hippocrates Prize for Poetry and Medicine, and the Cursed Murphy Spoken Word Award among others. Her writing residencies with the British Council, Literature Wales and Kultivera have seen her writing and performing poetry in Wales, Ireland, Sweden and India. She is the author of the poetry collections *And Suddenly You Find Yourself* and *Small* – both listed as Best Poetry Collections of the Year by *Wales Arts Review* – and, with Mari Ellis Dunning, the collaborative poetry pamphlet *The Wrong Side of the Looking Glass*. *Little Universe* is her third full collection.

How wearily you pull Kleenex from the packet,
stick figures springing backwards into hedgerows,
snowing pollen. How the world might not swallow you back.

The poems in Natalie Ann Holborow's third collection, *Little Universe*, are an exploration of tumultuous human emotions and nature's ever-present rhythms.

Lives bustle within a busy hospital's walls, humming against the Gower landscape that stretches beyond its windows. The tiny worlds of a wide cast unfold as they deal with their own emergencies, losses, recoveries, hopes and histories.

Medical students stride along the corridors in rubber shoes, scars running the lengths of their lives. A janitor is crying in the Gents, watching the flowers at the hospital entrance shrug themselves back into earth. The biblical Lilith offers knowledge from one woman to the other. And somewhere in the distance, a bunker dissolves into gold upon Pennard's shoulder, dusk folding to sleep on Rhossili.

The characters in this book are all bound by the undying pulse of existence – yet their stories serve as a reminder that despite these stark contrasts of grief and hope, life persists.

What inspired you to write *Little Universe*?
I started writing the book in 2020, a time when family members working in the NHS would be risking their lives going to work and my grandfather was diagnosed with cancer. In the same year, just weeks after my grandfather passed away, my little nephew Leo was born – the poem of the same title is about him. He's autistic and his routine of putting the planets in order soothes him, which inspired me to write the title poem. It's beautiful to watch him and learn how his little universe is different to mine.

It was a year of grief and hope, which became the book's main theme.

A lot of this book is set in Singleton Hospital, where I could see the comforting view of Swansea Bay through the window of my grandfather's room. This dichotomy of the fear of being inside hospital walls and the nature that ticks on outside the window has always felt somewhat profound. Even when attending diabetic clinic appointments, the sound of gulls on the hospital roof has become a comfort, reminding me of the Gower landscape outside the windows that I've loved since I was a child.

In 2020, so many of us reconnected with nature when our little universes were in turmoil. I want this book to remind people that they're not alone in grief and that there are still beautiful things in this chaotic world.

What is your writing process?

Running, walking and music are all central to my writing process. If I've got just a little glimmer of what might become a poem, there's nothing better than putting on my headphones and heading out to let those thoughts branch out into something bigger. It may mean stopping on the side of a path to tap notes into my phone, but it means I can return to my desk refreshed and inspired.

I pretty much listened to The Antlers' 'Kettering' track on repeat when I started writing this book. Devastating though it was, it just felt like a theme track to what I wanted to write. The poems started to play out like a film while I listened.

If I'm out running, I'm usually listening to something with an important message or theme for the first 5K. For the rest of it, I'm done mentally writing and it could be anything from Dolly Parton to Avenged Sevenfold.

This is why I am a writer and not a DJ.

What books are currently on your bedside table?

Too many. But the ones I'm picking up most at the moment are *Wilding* by Isabella Tree, *The Butterfly House* by Kathryn Bevis (this is a second-time-round read), *Bliss and Blunder* by Victoria Gosling and *Egg/Shell* by Victoria Kennefick.

There's always at least one fiction, one non-fiction and one or two poetry books on the go.

I call this a balanced book diet.

What advice would you give to your younger self?

All the time you're wasting worrying that people don't like you or that your work is terrible is time that you could be writing, reading and growing as a poet.

I still grapple with this now in my thirties, but I'm better at just writing despite it – I've realised that usually, it's me who's my most awful, non-constructive critic. I'd also tell myself to see feedback as gold dust and stop reacting sensitively. I've learned that if criticism is constructive, it's a stepping stone to growth. It's why I'm grateful to be friends with writers who offer honest and helpful advice when I need the truth.

Why do you write?
Because I feel. Because everyone feels. Books to me have always been a way of feeling less alone and of finding comfort, hope or inspiration. You never know who might need your words at a certain time. If there's something that needs to be said, the arts are the best way to connect with people and get that message across. It's why films, music and books have such an impact on people.

It's all about connection. And we need connection more than ever.

Natalie Ann Holborow, Autumn 2024

PARTHIAN *Poetry*

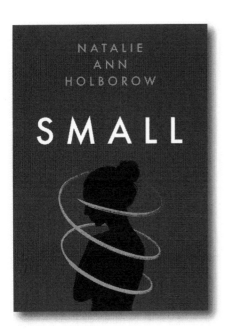

Small
Natalie Ann Holborow
ISBN 978-1-912681-76-1
£9.99 | Paperback

'Any woman will tell you that loving our bodies is a challenge, but Small reminds us that if women could, we could set this whole place on fire.'
– Zoë Brigley

We all have our favourite demons. Weaved throughout poems on mythology, literary figures and other shores, the narrator is haunted by her biggest demon of all: the gargantuan Small. Told with rawness and honesty, the secretive nature of living with an eating disorder is yanked out into the open and given physical form and voice.

This Common Uncommon
Rae Howells
ISBN 978-1-914595-90-5
£10.00 | Paperback

'Finely wrought, intelligent, and full of heart... [This Common Uncommon is] an important book that speaks for nature, land, and species which, too often, we see as silent: a vital tome at a time of urgency.'
– Mab Jones, *Buzz Magazine*

When a local common is threatened with development, one poet explores its secrets, discovering extraordinary natural treasures and wonderful people fighting to defend them. Can they save this uncommon common?

'It's a delight to share her excitement at being in, and her care for, the natural world' – *The Friday Poem*

This Common Uncommon
Rae Howells
'these poems capture the unique character of our wonderful common' – Susan Cole

PARTHIAN *Poetry*

Wild Cherry: Selected Poems
Nigel Jenkins

ISBN 978-1-914595-22-6
£10.00 | Paperback

'He became the unacknowledged national poet of his generation, an open-hearted soul whose poems embodied much of what our nation is today – diverse, passionate, tender and unafraid to take a hard look at its political and cultural complexity.'
– Menna Elfyn

'Nigel Jenkins has a staggering presence in the literature of Wales. His poetry was both political and beautiful, deeply human, wonderfully cosmological and often scathingly humorous. Swansea's most amiable bard and, undoubtedly, its most popular poet since Dylan Thomas.'
– Tôpher Mills

Moon Jellyfish Can Barely Swim
Ness Owen

ISBN 978-1-913640-97-2
£10.00 | Paperback

'Form and feeling combine to create a collection which rewards the reader with a mesmerising portrait of a much-loved landscape brimming with startling imagery.'
– Samantha Wynne-Rhydderch

Moon jellyfish live a life adrift. Owen's second collection explores what it is to subsist with whatever the tides bring. Poems that journey from family to politics, womanhood and language.